D1243452

Esports and the New Gaming Culture

Bradley Steffens

San Diego, CA

For more information, contact:
ReferencePoint Press, Inc.
PO Box 27779
San Diego, CA 92198
www.ReferencePointPress.com

LIBRARY OF CONGRESS CATALOGING-IN-PUBLICATION DATA

Names: Steffens, Bradley, 1955- author.
Title: Esports and the new gaming culture / by Bradley Steffens.
Description: San Diego, CA : ReferencePoint Press Inc., 2021. | Includes
    bibliographical references and index.
Identifiers: LCCN 2020015968 (print) | LCCN 2020015969 (ebook) | ISBN
    9781682829257 (library binding) | ISBN 9781682829264 (ebook)
Subjects: LCSH: eSports (Contests)--Juvenile literature.
Classification: LCC GV1469.34.E86 S84 2021 (print) | LCC GV1469.34.E86
    (ebook) | DDC 794.8--dc23
LC record available at https://lccn.loc.gov/2020015968
LC ebook record available at https://lccn.loc.gov/2020015969

Contents

Important Events in the World of Esports

2000
The Korean Ministry of Culture, Sports and Tourism forms the Korean e-Sports Association.

1972
Stanford University students hold the first known collegiate video game tournament for the combat game *Spacewar!*

2005
The Cyberathlete Professional League World Tour holds a series of tournaments for *Painkiller* with a $1 million prize pool.

1990
Thousands of gamers compete in *Super Mario Bros.*, *Rad Racer*, and *Tetris* in the first Nintendo World Championships.

1975	1985	1995	2005

1997
Microsoft sponsors the Red Annihilation tournament for the popular first-person shooter game *Quake*. Winner Dennis "Thresh" Fong receives a 1987 Ferrari 328 GTS as the grand prize.

1980
Atari holds the first large-scale video game tournament: the National Space Invaders Championship.

2002
Sundance DiGiovanni and Mike Sepso found the Major League Gaming Corporation to hold official video game tournaments throughout the United States and Canada.

2009
The Collegiate Starleague launches its first *StarCraft* tournament with twenty-five participating schools.

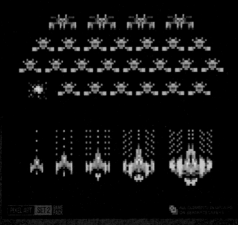

2011
Video game publisher Valve launches the International, an annual esports world championship tournament for *Dota 2*.

2017
PlayVS forms an exclusive partnership with the National Federation of State High School Associations to provide a framework for high school esports.

2014
Robert Morris University becomes the first higher education institution to offer *League of Legends* scholarships.

2020
Due to the COVID-19 pandemic, dozens of in-person esports events were canceled or postponed, but many high school, college, and professional leagues continued to hold competitions with players competing from remote locations.

2010   **2015**   **2020**   **2025**

2012
Blizzard Entertainment launches the *StarCraft II* World Championship Series.

2016
The National Association of Collegiate Esports is founded.

2019
Sixteen-year-old Kyle "Bugha" Giersdorf takes home the $3 million prize for winning the inaugural *Fortnite* World Cup.

2018
Fédération Internationale de l'Automobile launches the FIA *Gran Turismo* Championship.

2013
The US government recognizes *League of Legends* as a professional sport, allowing foreign players to receive visas to enter the United States to play in tournaments.

Introduction

A Human Drama

Intently watching his family's flat screen TV on August 25, 2019, John Jewell Balan, a student at Celtech College in San Fernando, Philippines, suddenly leaped to his feet and pumped his fist as his favorite team overcame an early deficit and took the lead in the final game of the championship series. A power forward on an amateur basketball team, Balan was not watching a National Basketball Association (NBA) final or any traditional sports competition. He was one of 48 million people worldwide watching the Grand Final of the International, a video game tournament in which eighteen teams played the battle arena game *Dota 2*, vying for the top prize of $15.6 million. It was the largest prize in the history of professional video game competitions, which are the most significant aspect of the world of electronic sports, or more popularly, esports. In all, an average audience of 23 million people watched 122 hours of the tournament over 5 days, for a total of more than 2.8 billion viewer hours, according to Esports Charts, a media analytics company. Balan, who plays *Dota 2* at a video game lounge near the Celtech campus, was captivated by the nonstop action and split-second strategic moves of the professional gamers. "These players are amazing," he says. "I love their teamwork and never-say-die-until-you-win attitude."[1]

As popular as the International is, it is not the biggest esports tournament in the world. According to Esports Charts, the 2018 *League of Legends* World Championship finals had 205 million

peak viewers (including viewers in China)—almost five times the number of the International's peak audience. An average of 47 million viewers watched 132 million hours of the *League of Legends* World Championship for a total of 6.2 billion viewer hours.

All in all, 454 million people watched esports on television and online in 2019, an increase of 15 percent over 2018. More people watch esports than Netflix, Hulu, ESPN, and HBO put together.

Fans watch the action live at the League of Legends *World Championship finals in Spain in 2019.*

The 2019 *League of Legends* World Championship finals drew 105 million viewers (excluding China), according to Business Insider. For comparison, the 2019 Super Bowl had just over 98 million viewers. Esports has surpassed golf and rugby to become the ninth most-watched sport in the world.

A Financial Gold Mine

The global popularity of esports has drawn the attention of businesses looking to profit from the burgeoning industry. Video game publishers, who create and market the games, are investing hundreds of millions of dollars to sponsor tournaments promoting their most popular games. Television networks and media companies are spending tens of millions of dollars to obtain the broadcast and streaming rights to the biggest events. Advertisers, who are always looking for new ways to reach young consumers, are sponsoring teams, broadcasts, and livestreams of tournaments and even player practice sessions on video streaming platforms, including YouTube, Twitch, and Mixer. Merchandisers are marketing T-shirts, hoodies, shoes, and other branded gear to esports fans. Total global revenues for esports surpassed $1 billion in 2019.

The vast amount of money being generated by esports has attracted the interest of investors who want to become team owners. Some, like Robert Kraft, owner of the National Football League's (NFL) New England Patriots, have already succeeded as owners of sports teams. Others, like retired New York Yankees infielder Alex Rodriguez and former Los Angeles Laker Shaquille O'Neal, are successful former athletes who thrive on the thrill of competition. Some, like recording artists Drake, Sean "Diddy" Combs, and Jennifer Lopez, are celebrities who are looking for new ways to connect to the young audiences that fuel their careers.

Educational Opportunity

Educators are also looking at esports as a way to reach young people. In the past, video gaming was something educators discouraged because it was believed to have negative effects on academic achievement. Now colleges, high schools, and even middle schools are embracing e-sports as a healthy addition to academic life. "Esports has tremendous potential, both to inspire students to learn 21st-century skills and also to include many students who have previously been marginalized with respect to competitive activities,"[2] says Donald Brinkman, a senior program manager at Microsoft.

> "Esports has tremendous potential, both to inspire students to learn 21st-century skills and also to include many students who have previously been marginalized with respect to competitive activities."[2]
>
> —Donald Brinkman, senior program manager at Microsoft

Christopher Turner, an art teacher and esports coach at Southern University Laboratory School in Baton Rouge, Louisiana, sees esports as a way to harness the passion of student gamers. "This was something they did that was fun, but now they can benefit from so much by being in this league," Turner says. "Studies have shown that they can also develop STEM (science, technology, engineering and mathematics) skills. They can also learn about computer codes and game development. This will give them so many opportunities."[3]

The Real Deal

Despite all the excitement generated by esports, some people question whether it should be considered a sport at all, since it does not involve a significant degree of physical athleticism. "It's not a sport—it's a competition," says John Skipper, president of ESPN, the cable television network devoted to traditional sports. "Chess is a competition. Checkers is a competition."[4]

Esports fans like Balan disagree. They feel the same surge of excitement that traditional sports fans do—the thrill that comes from watching a fast-paced struggle between two evenly matched opponents, where the game and its strategies are well understood but the outcome is unknown—a human drama played out in real time. And they know from playing the games themselves that pro gamers possess physical and mental skills far beyond their own, including freakishly fast reflexes, extraordinary hand-eye coordination, and an uncanny awareness of what is happening all around the video screen. Elite gamers also have immense powers of concentration, able to remain focused on a complex, ever-changing field of play for hours at a time. And as Balan noted, the best esports players possess a deep desire to win, an unwavering commitment to come out on top, no matter how desperate things may get or how hopeless they may seem. They persevere. As champions do.

Chapter One

A Global Phenomenon

Things looked bleak for OG, a *Dota 2* professional team based in Europe, as the 2018 edition of the International's 2018 tournament approached. Earlier in the year, OG star Anathan "ana" Pham decided to take a break from competitive gaming. Without ana, the team struggled through one tournament after another. Then Tal "Fly" Aizik, an Israeli Canadian professional, and Gustav "s4" Magnusson, a Swedish professional, both left OG to join Evil Geniuses, a rival esports team based in the United States. Despite having won several tournaments in the past, OG was so weakened in 2018 that it was not invited to the International or even to the regional qualifier. If OG was going to participate in the International, it would have to do it the hard way, earning a spot through the open qualifying rounds.

Cinderella Story

Just before the tournament began, ana returned to OG. He was joined by Topias Miikka "Topson" Taavitsainen, a Finnish professional *Dota 2* player. The team swept through open qualifying and secured a spot in the regional qualifier. In regionals, OG did not lose a single game, and the team qualified for the main tournament.

The tournament did not start well for OG. Playing in Group A, the Europeans managed to take one game off tournament favorites PSG.LGD, a team from China, but were defeated 2–1. On the second day, OG was swept 2–0 by defending champions Team Liquid of the Netherlands. However, facing elimination on the third day, OG rallied to win five games and lose only one. The winning spree put OG into the tournament's final four.

Group B winner VGJ.Storm, a North American squad, chose to play OG in the first round of the finals, believing OG to be the weakest of the four finalists. However, OG shocked their opponents, defeating them in two straight games. OG then went up against Evil Geniuses and their former teammates Fly and s4. The best-of-three series came down to the final game, and OG again surprised the experts by defeating their rival. The win put OG in the upper bracket against PSG.LGD, the team that had defeated them 2–1 in the playoffs.

The teams split the first two games, but in the third game PSG.LGD took control by eliminating ana's hero, Spectre. As PSG.LGD moved in on OG's Ancient to end the game, Topson fought back with his hero, Zet, the Arc Warden, singlehandedly repulsing three attackers. Topson then led a pulse-pounding counterattack against the retreating PSG.LGD forces, culminating in a successful attack on PSG.LGD's Ancient, ending the game.

> "Against all odds, we stood united, fought until the very end and became your #TI8 Champions! The Dream is now real."[5]
>
> —OG team, *Dota 2* champions in 2018

The Grand Final was a rematch with PSG.LGD. For only the second time in the International's history, the Grand Final went the full five games. After splitting the first four games, PSG.LGD took a commanding lead in the fifth game, mainly through successful deployment of the hero Earthshaker. But, as before, when things looked their worst, OG fought back. Using superior team fighting tactics, OG overcame the deficit and claimed the Aegis of Champions trophy and $11 million in prize money. "Against all odds, we stood united, fought until the very end and

A man watches the 2018 International Dota 2 esport games online. The event drew 15 million online viewers in 2018 and more than tripled the number of viewers in 2019.

became your #TI8 Champions!" stated the team on Twitter. "The Dream is now real."[5]

OG's 2018 Cinderella story was viewed by nearly 20,000 people who attended the matches at the Rogers Arena in Vancouver, Canada, and by another 15 million people who watched online and on cable and satellite television. As popular as the 2018 tournament was, the number of people watching the championship game more than tripled the next year, when 48 million people watched the 2019 edition of the International, according to Esports Charts. In that tournament, OG shocked the world again when it became the first team in the history of the International to win back-to-back championships.

The International is just one of eight major *Dota 2* tournaments held each year. In addition, there are another eighteen smaller *Dota 2* professional tournaments held throughout the year in as many as twelve different countries. But *Dota 2*, published by American

The Ten Most Popular Games on Twitch

Digital research firm Newzoo continuously tracks live viewing and streaming behavior across Twitch and then ranks the top games on a monthly basis by total hours watched (in millions). Newzoo tracks both esports hours—hours of content from professionally organized esports competitions—and total overall hours, which adds individual player streams to the esports total. Its rankings also show the percentage of the total hours that comes from sanctioned esports alone, which can be high, as in the case of Tom Clancy's *Rainbow Six: Siege* or low, as with *Fortnite*. The rankings below are from February 2020.

Game	Total Hours	Esports Hours	Share Esports
1. *League of Legends*	119.5M	14.6M	12.2%
2. *Fortnite*	54.3M	0.0M	0.0%
3. *Counter-Strike: Global Offensive*	49.4M	18.3M	37.2%
4. *Escape from Tarkov*	48.0M	0.0M	0.0%
5. *Grand Theft Auto V*	42.6M	0.0M	0.0%
6. *Dota 2*	34.6M	6.8M	19.7%
7. *World of Warcraft*	31.3M	0.0M	0.0%
8. *Apex Legends*	27.8M	0.2M	0.5%
9. *Hearthstone*	18.9M	0.1M	0.6%
10. Tom Clancy's *Rainbow Six: Siege*	17.4M	8.0M	46.2%

Newzoo, "Most Watched Games on Twitch," February 2020. https://newzoo.com.

video game developer Valve, is just one of many gaming platforms that make up the esports universe. In fact, Valve publishes two other games—*Counter-Strike* and *Team Fortress*—that are also played at the professional level.

Multiplayer Online Battle Arena Games

In all, at least forty different games are played professionally. These are divided into eight categories. *Dota 2* is categorized as a multiplayer online battle arena game. Games in this category involve teams of individual players, each of whom controls a single hero, as they battle for control of an arena—typically a world represented by a three-dimensional map viewed from a raised perspective, known as an isometric perspective. Other games in this category include *Heroes of the Storm*, *League of Legends*, *Mobile Legends: Bang Bang*, *Smite*, and *Vainglory*.

With *League of Legends* and *Dota 2* in the lineup, the multiplayer online battle arena category is one of the most popular in all of esports. The twenty-three thousand tickets for the 2018 *League of Legends* world final in South Korea sold out in less than four hours upon their release, even though the tournament was broadcast online. The world finals in 2017, held in Beijing's Olympic Bird's Nest stadium, drew a sold-out crowd of forty thousand.

Real-Time Strategy Games

Multiplayer online battle arena games grew out of an older but still popular category of games: real-time strategy games. In these games, a player or team typically builds bases, gathers resources, and produces units to conquer enemies and take control of a map, while their opponents are doing the same thing at the same time. Winning requires the players to think strategically about what needs to be done and how to do it. The major real-time strategy game played professionally is *StarCraft II*.

At one time, *StarCraft II* was the biggest esports game on the planet, with dozens of tournaments being played around the world. "'StarCraft II' really started the modern era of esports," says Adrian Harris, a video game executive who headed up the

> "'StarCraft II' really started the modern era of esports."[6]
>
> —Adrian Harris, video game executive

StarCraft esports program. "We had this period between 2010 and 2012 when we were the only kid on the block. I remember being at IPL4 [a multi-game competition held in Las Vegas], where 'League of Legends' had this tiny side stage, and saying 'What's this game?!'"[6] Other games overtook *StarCraft II*, although many fans stayed loyal to the game, especially in South Korea. Every winner of the *StarCraft* World Championship from 2012 to 2017 was from South Korea. The streak ended in 2018, when Joona "Serral" Sotala of Finland took home the big prize. "Yess!! Managed to pull it off 4–3!!! Dream come true,"[7] tweeted Sotala.

In 2020 the game's publisher, Activision Blizzard, ended the World Championship Series. It announced that it would fund a new *StarCraft* professional league that would be managed by ESL, a German esports organizing company, and DreamHack, a Swedish production company specializing in esports tournaments.

Shooter Games

Shooter games also grew out of some of the oldest computer games and remain one of the most popular genres in both home entertainment and professional esports. There are two kinds of shooter games, with some overlap: first-person shooter games and third-person shooter games.

In first-person shooter games, the player views the action through the eyes of a single person, the protagonist. Often, the protagonist's arms extend into view from the bottom of the screen, holding whatever shooting weapon the character is using. As the player advances through the game, the shooter's-eye view often rocks from side to side, mimicking the human gait. With the first-person perspective and the sounds of footsteps and breathing, the game puts the player into the virtual world. The character's location is often shown on a small map on the screen. The player shoots and eliminates enemies as the protagonist proceeds toward a goal. The most popular first-person shooter pro games include *Battlefield*, *Call of Duty*, *Counter-Strike*, *CrossFire*, *Doom II*, *Halo*, *Overwatch*, *Rainbow Six: Siege*, *Special Force II*, and *Team Fortress 2*. First-person shooters are very common in competition events.

Third-person shooter games are similar, but the point of view is from above and behind the protagonist. Instead of viewing the action through the protagonist's eyes, the player sees an avatar of the protagonist moving and shooting. This allows the protagonist to be better defined and more interesting to look at. As a result, following the action is like watching a movie. However, the third-person perspective makes aiming the weapon more difficult. The two kinds of games can overlap because third-person games often allow the shooter to switch to a first-person point of view for more precise shooting. First-person games sometimes switch to third-person point of view when the shooter is in a vehicle. The most successful third-person shooter games are *Gears of War*, *Fortnite*, and *PlayerUnknown's Battlegrounds*.

Some third-person games are used in competition. For example, *Gears of War* pits

A gamer plays a third-person shooter game. Instead of viewing the action through the protagonist's eyes, the player sees an avatar of the protagonist moving and shooting.

a team of human players against two virtual enemies: the Locust Horde and the Lambent. The fourth installment in the series has a popular team-versus-team playing mode. In 2016 Xbox, which controls the rights to *Gears of War*, launched the Gears eSports Pro Circuit for *Gears of War 4*. Managed by Major League Gam-

A Teenage Pro Gamer Balances Practice and School

Kyle "Bugha" Giersdorf won the 2019 *Fortnite* World Cup and its $3 million prize at age sixteen, when he was still a student at Pottsgrove High School in Pottsgrove, Pennsylvania. He discusses how he strikes a balance between gaming and school:

> I started playing about two years ago and I think when I first started playing competitively was around, maybe, a year after I started playing. . . .
>
> I [practice], on average, six hours. Usually on school days, I start around 3 and end around 9. So when I get home around 2, I have an hour to do [home]work, and later at 9, I have another hour to do work. . . .
>
> [My parents] were skeptical about the amount of time I was putting into the game because they thought I was missing out on some other aspects of life, but once they realized it could be an actual career, they started supporting me a little bit more. . . .
>
> I think one of the most important things is to stay confident. You definitely want to put a lot of your time improving certain aspects, like going over what you do wrong and how to improve from that. . . .
>
> I'm definitely just going to save the money and invest it into my future. . . .
>
> I just want to keep competing, striving to get better. Also, want to grow my Twitch channel, my YouTube, my social [network pages]. All that.

Quoted in Katie Park, "Meet 'Bugha,' the Pennsylvania Teen Who Won the *Fortnite* World Cup's $3 Million Prize," *Philadelphia (PA) Inquirer*, August 1, 2019. www.inquirer.com.

ing and Gfinity, the pro circuit features live open events around the world, with players competing for $1 million in cash prizes.

Battle Royale–Style Games

The two other major third-person shooter games, *Fortnite* and *PlayerUnknown's Battlegrounds* (*PUBG*), are battle royale–style games. In these games, an individual competes against up to ninety-nine other players to be the sole survivor on the battlefield—an area that shrinks as the game progresses, bringing the players into greater proximity with each other. The players must scavenge for vital supplies while eliminating the other competitors.

The battle royale genre is the brainchild of Brendan "PlayerUnknown" Greene, who developed battle modules for military simulators. Released in 2017, *PUBG* became one of the most popular games in history, selling more than 50 million copies worldwide by June 2018, with over 400 million players. Professional *PUBG* matches pit sixteen squads of four players against each other. The pro gamers are required to play in first-person perspective mode only. The *PUBG* Global Championship 2019 offered a prize pool of $4 million, with $2 million going to the four members of the winning team, Gen.G Esports.

Fortnite is also one of the world's biggest esports games, with more than 250 million players registered around the world. The 2019 *Fortnite* World Cup, which offered $30 million in prizes, was open to any registered player. More than 40 million players across the globe participated in the tournament. The finals, held in New York City, were the culmination of ten weeks of elimination rounds. Kyle "Bugha" Giersdorf, a sixteen-year-old gamer from Pennsylvania, was crowned the World Cup solo winner and was awarded $3 million.

Fighting Games

Not all combat games involve shooting. Hand-to-hand combat games, known as fighting games, are some of the most popular esports contests. *Killer Instinct*, *Marvel vs. Capcom*, *Street*

Fighter, *Super Smash Bros.*, and *Tekken* are the biggest fighting games on the pro circuit. The concept is simple: the player chooses a character from a roster of fighters and battles an opponent one-on-one.

There are many fighting game tournaments throughout the year, but the biggest and longest running is the Evolution Championship Series tournament in the United States. The 2019 festival featured *Street Fighter V*, *Tekken 7*, *BlazBlue: Cross Tag Battle*, *Dragon Ball FighterZ*, *Mortal Kombat 11*, *Soulcalibur VI*, *Under Night In-Birth Exe: Late[st]*, *Samurai Shodown*, and *Super Smash Bros*.

Super Smash Bros. was the most popular game of the event, attracting 58,000 average viewers, with a peak viewership of 245,000. The number of hours watched reached a total of 1.7 million. The *Super Smash Bros. Ultimate* tournament had 3,534 entrants—a record for *Smash* tournaments—who competed for the $35,290 prize.

Sports Games

By simulating hand-to-hand combat, fighting games are similar to actual human sports such as karate and fencing. Games in the category of esports known as sports games go even further, closely simulating popular professional sports, including Fédération Internationale de Football Association (FIFA) soccer, NFL Football, and NBA basketball. The most popular games in this category are *FIFA*, *Madden NFL*, *NBA 2K*, *Pro Evolution Soccer*, and *Rocket League*. All these games except for *Rocket League* use computer-generated images of human athletes to create realistic sports situations on the gaming screen. (In *Rocket League*, players compete at soccer using animated rocket-powered cars.) The computer graphics are so detailed that even the player interactions—two players wrestling over a ball, for example—appear real. The goal is to create the illusion that the gamer is on the field or court.

Launched as *John Madden Football* in 1988, *Madden NFL* is one of the oldest sports games in the world. Named after Super

Oakland Raiders' head coach John Madden is carried off the field by his players after winning the Super Bowl in 1977. Named after the popular coach, EA Sports' Madden NFL 20 *video game* has sold 130 million copies.

Bowl–winning coach John Madden of the Oakland Raiders, the game has sold 130 million copies. In 1993 the game's publisher, EA Sports, struck a deal with the NFL to allow it to use NFL teams and players in the video game, making the game even more appealing to NFL fans. In addition, NFL announcers "call" the games using prerecorded sound bites. With $4 billion in sales, *Madden NFL* is now the NFL's second-largest revenue stream, after the merchandising of NFL clothing and gear.

The first *Madden NFL* tournament—the *Madden* Bowl—was held in 1995. In April 2019 twenty-year-old Drini Gjoka, playing as the Dallas Cowboys, won the 2019 *Madden* Bowl over eighteen-year-old runner-up Michael Spoto, playing as the New York Giants.

After building up a 31–0 halftime lead, Gjoka, wearing his trademark camouflage bandana, cruised to a 41–0 victory, taking home the *Madden* Championship Series belt and $40,000 first prize. It was the second championship for Gjoka, who won the 2017 *Madden* Bowl at age eighteen, becoming the youngest winner in the tournament's history. "Thanks to everyone who has helped me get to this point," Gjoka said on Twitter after the win. "Words can't explain how I feel right now."[8]

Racing Games

Race car driving is another real-life sport that has virtual counterparts in the esports world. In fact, several professional auto racing organizations have endorsed and sponsored the esports competitions. For example, in 2010 the National Association for Stock Car Auto Racing (NASCAR) launched the eNASCAR iRacing World Championship Series. Then in 2019 NASCAR teamed up with developer 704Games to launch the eNASCAR Heat Pro League, with a total prize pool of $200,000.

The best-known auto racing esport is the FIA *Gran Turismo* Championship. Launched in 2018, the tournament is sponsored by Fédération Internationale de l'Automobile, the governing body for many auto racing events, including the well-known Formula One races. Finalists from the prior year compete with newcomers who qualify via the Online Series, which runs for several months. Brazilian gamer Igor Fraga won the first two editions of the *Gran Turismo* Sport's Nations Cup Final, the first time when he was twenty years old. The other major auto racing tournaments are the Project CARS Electronic Sports League and the TrackMania Championship Series.

Other Games

Some of the most popular esports games do not fit into a single category. These include *Hearthstone*, *Pokémon*, *Puyo Puyo*, *Te-*

tris, *War Thunder*, *World of Tanks*, and *World of Warcraft*. *Poké-mon* has tournaments for four different games, all based on the popular characters and stories from the card game. *Tetris* and *Puyo Puyo* are both tile-matching puzzle games that have been adapted to esports viewing. *World of Tanks* and *War Thunder* are multiplayer vehicular combat games, featuring tanks and other machines of war.

The *World of Tanks* tournament features fourteen eight-person teams battling for a steel trophy called the Monolith and a $300,000 prize. *World of Warcraft* is a massively multiplayer online role-playing game. First released in 2004, *World of Warcraft* is played by 10 million people worldwide. The game's biggest esports tournament, the Battle for Azeroth Finals, features a prize pool of $500,000.

Fifteen million esports fans watch video game content daily on Twitch and YouTube. The vast majority are gamers themselves. Some watch to pick up strategies and tips that will help their own game play. Others are entertained by watching players with superior skills competing against each other. And still others are loyal fans of certain teams and players and enjoy following their progress through the season, ranks, and tournaments. Almost all feel a camaraderie with the players and other fans. They talk about it with their friends, fellow students, and coworkers. Esports is a group activity that makes the fans feel part of something bigger than themselves. It is the national pastime of a new generation.

Chapter Two

Inside the World of Pro Gamers

Players are the foundation of esports. Video games may have amazing graphics, challenging goals, fascinating characters, and creative story lines, but without players, they are simply software programs waiting to be used. It is the player's decisions, reactions, and strategies that bring the game to life and make it exciting to watch.

Likewise, esports teams, leagues, streaming platforms, and television broadcasts only exist because there are players who are so exceptional at what they do that hundreds of millions of people want to watch them. Because talented gamers are at the center of the industry, they can earn money playing the game—in some cases a great deal of money. But part of turning pro involves sacrifices and compromises. In addition, there are pressures to perform well—from team owners, sponsors, and fans. It is not just a job; it is a lifestyle.

From Amateur to Pro

Most pro gamers start out by making a name for themselves in local tournaments. "Once you reach the top of a competition, you think maybe I can take this to another level where I can turn my hobby into a profession,"[9] says Peter "ppd" Dager, a member of the professional *Dota 2* team Ninjas in Pyjamas. In tournaments, a player's skills can attract the attention of a pro team that is looking to add a new player. This is how Sasha "Scarlett" Hostyn, a Canadian pro gamer who is the first woman to win a major *StarCraft II* tournament, was recruited to the pro ranks.

Scarlett started playing *StarCraft II* when she was eleven. She credits her brother for encouraging her to consider playing professionally. "My brother watched a lot of *Starcraft II*, pro matches, so I guess he got me into it," she explains. "I just got really good at it when I was playing for fun, so I tried playing a few tournaments and just went from there."[10]

When she was eighteen, Scarlett entered an online female-only tournament, the NESL Iron Lady, and won. In 2012 she won the Playhem "Sponsor Me!" Tournament, an online event designed to help amateur players find a team or a sponsor. As part of the winner's award, she received a sponsored trip to the IGN ProLeague Season 4, a tournament in Las Vegas, Nevada. Scarlett participated in the open bracket and won the first two games over two well-known players, Terius and DdoRo. She lost in the third round and dropped down to the loser's bracket. But there she pulled another upset by defeating DeMusliM 2–0, knocking him out of the tournament. She lost her next match, but her excellent play brought her to the attention of Eclypsia, an international team located in France. The team offered Scarlett a contract, and her pro career took off. She has played for several teams, including Dead Pixels, Team Expert, Tollenz Lions, and Newbee. Guinness World Records lists Scarlett as having the highest career earnings for a female competitive video game player, with more than $271,000 in winnings.

Ryan "OpTicJ" Musselman, a founding member of OpTic Gaming, a four-time *Call of Duty* Major League Gaming champion

> "I just got really good at it when I was playing for fun, so I tried playing a few tournaments and just went from there."[10]
>
> —Sasha "Scarlett" Hostyn, first woman to win a major *StarCraft II* tournament

Sasha "Scarlett" Hostyn (on right) is a Canadian pro gamer who is the first woman to win a major StarCraft II tournament. She started playing StarCraft II when she was eleven.

team, took a more direct route into the professional ranks. He was a member of a nonprofessional team called Cereal Killers that kept losing to a better team known as Dog Company. One day, Musselman went online and saw the Dog Company leader Casey "OpTic KR3W" Barton playing another member of his team. Calling himself Willy Jones, Musselman jumped into the game. He remembers:

They were playing on a map called Vossenack. It's a very small map, usually used when players wanted to settle a 1v1 [one-on-one] sniper challenge. Once I saw them in there, I pulled out a sniper rifle and just started tearing them apart. That got their attention, so I asked Casey if they were holding tryouts. It was kind of a joke at first, but he was cool about it. He said, "If you can beat us, you can join." So I started beating them, and as promised, they invited me to join the team.[11]

Living in a Gaming House

Playing on a professional team is a full-time commitment. Most elite teams require the players to live together in what is known as a gaming house. The young adult players eat together, work out together, and of course practice together—at least six hours a day. Gaming houses started appearing in the early 2000s in South Korea, when *StarCraft: Brood War* players Lim "BoxeR" Yo Hwan and Hong "YellOw" Jin-ho moved in together. The practice spread throughout South Korea and China, and finally to the West. "Gaming houses were, in my eyes, a requirement," says Team Liquid chief operating officer Mike Milanov. "There were some teams that had everyone remote, and then they would have to fly every Friday and waste that time to fly to [Los Angeles], then compete Saturday, Sunday, then Sunday night, fly back. People were losing practice, they were losing development, they were losing team bonding."[12]

The typical gaming house includes a practice room with state-of-the-art gaming equipment, a gym, a swimming pool, and recreational equipment like a Ping-Pong table, soccer net, basketball hoop, and even cornhole boards. Los Angeles–based Ghost Gaming has a team house overlooking Hollywood with ten beds and sixteen bathrooms for the ten-person team. Older players often have their own bedrooms, while younger players may bunk together. The kitchen is staffed with a personal chef to prepare lunch and dinner. A maid service keeps the gaming home clean. Essentially, all the pro gamers have to do is eat, sleep, take care of themselves, and play their game. "When most people just take a quick look at the house we're living in, it's a bunch of teenagers, and it's a lot of us, so you would think it's rowdy, we're just reckless, but we're professional e-sports players,"[13] says former Ghost Gaming player Michael "SpaceLy" Schmale.

To ensure the house serves its purpose, which is to make sure the team members can give their peak performances in their

> "I started beating them, and as promised, they invited me to join the team."[11]
>
> —OpTicJ, founding member of OpTic Gaming team

To foster player development and bonding, most elite teams require players to live together in a gaming house that includes a practice room with state-of-the-art gaming equipment, a gym, and a swimming pool.

matches, it has a structured schedule that the players follow. At the Ghost Gaming mansion, the players wake up between 9:00 a.m. and 9:30 a.m., have breakfast, and report to the gym at 11:00 a.m. Personal trainers guide them through a rigorous workout that lasts from an hour to an hour and a half. The players then meet up in the film room to review their own performances and to watch what other teams do. They break for lunch and then move to the practice area, put on their headsets, and play from 1:30 p.m. to 7:30 p.m. "That's just a long grind of playing against other talented teams,"[14] Schmale explains. After practice is another chef-prepared dinner that can include high-end specialties such as lobster. The goal, says Milanov, is to keep the players healthy.

The evenings are set aside for relaxation. The players have access to vehicles—including Lamborghinis and other luxury cars—but they rarely use them. "They'll practice for six, seven, eight hours a day, just like you and I would go to work," says Hung Tran, marketing and content director for the Philadelphia Fusion, a professional Philadelphia-based team that plays *Overwatch*. But after that, most players hang out in the gaming house. "They're gamers," says Tran. "They just want to play games on the side."[15] Many pro gamers have large, paid followings on YouTube, Twitch, or Mixer, and they stream their individual play at night. If they miss a session, they might lose subscribers.

Revenue Streams

Subscribers are important to pro gamers because their salaries are not extravagant. The average salary for an esports player is about $50,000 a year. Unlike most workers, however, pro gamers who live in gaming houses do not have to spend any of their salary for housing, utilities, or food. They also do not pay for travel and lodging expenses when the team competes in tournaments that take place out of town. The team takes care of those expenses, too.

In addition, esports team members split tournament winnings among themselves. For example, when OG won the International in 2019, the five-member team split the $15,578,510 top prize, with each player's share of the prize coming in at $3.1 million. This was the largest individual payout to a single esports player in history, and it put all five OG team members at the top of the esports individual player earnings for 2019. Esports players received more than $211 million in prize pool money in 2019.

A Tenuous Position

Although pro gamers make a comfortable living, their status is insecure. Players can be and often are dropped from the roster with little warning. A poor performance in a tournament, a conflict with other team members, or simply the availability of a better player can lead a team to release one of its members. For example, Schmale spent only six months with Ghost Gaming, from June 2017 to January 2018, before being dropped. He was philosophical about his release:

> This sounds very tragic and could nearly end a player's career, but this is a very common thing in the scene. Players get released and switched around all the time. My advice to young gamers that want to play professionally: You gotta stay patient. You gotta stay dedicated. And understand that it's gonna take sacrifice, because there's always another person out there trying to take that spot. But I don't have any plans to give up the gaming career. I'm gonna bounce back from this and make my mom and dad proud.[16]

Bounce back he did, signing with PURE Gaming, another American esports team, within a month. In all, Schmale played for thirty-five teams from 2011 to 2020.

Lifestyle Gamers

The lack of security in competitive gaming is one of the reasons that some pro gamers leave their teams or never join one in the first place. Instead, they concentrate their efforts on building up a following on video streaming platforms like YouTube, Twitch, and Mixer. These players are known as lifestyle gamers. They are not active competitors; they are entertainers. They do more

"My advice to young gamers that want to play professionally: You gotta stay patient. You gotta stay dedicated. And understand that it's gonna take sacrifice, because there's always another person out there trying to take that spot."[16]

—Michael "SpaceLy" Schmale, pro gamer

Ali "Myth" Kabbani

Born on May 24, 1999, to Syrian and African American parents, Ali Kabbani, known in the esports world as Myth, has 5.8 million followers on Twitch and 4.37 million subscribers on YouTube. A top-tier *Fortnite* player on Team SoloMid, Myth is known for his innovative strategies, his outstanding building skills, and his entertaining commentary as he plays. He talks about his career and some of the adversities he has overcome:

> I don't live in a community where what I do is heavily accepted. . . . That pressure from family. I took a very different route when it came to just life in general. Right out of high school I was like I wanna stream. That was something that was super risky and probably wasn't the best decision to be quite honest, but I kind of took that with an insane drive. I didn't think about failure. I just kind of went for it. . . .

> My mom was watching me on TV . . . or watching like my highlight videos. I remember waking up one morning, I walk out of my room and I hear like the audio or the video, and I'm like, "Is this what is happening? Is this real life right now?" . . .

> If I could, you know, make somebody's day. Show somebody that things don't always have to be dark as they may seem. Help people work on themselves. Being a positive light for people, I think, is something that influences me heavily.

Quoted in TheNetline, "TheMyth Biography," 2020. https://thenetline.com.

than excel at gaming. They cultivate an image as they talk to the audience while they play.

Lifestyle gamers earn most of their money from subscriptions to their video channels and advertisements served up before, during, and after they stream. Both Twitch and Mixer charge viewers around $5 a month to watch a particular gamer's channel ad free.

Ninja

One of the best-known lifestyle gamers is Tyler "Ninja" Blevins, a former competitive *Halo* player who now plays *Fortnite* for millions of followers. Ninja earns about $10 million a year from paid subscriptions, advertising on his YouTube channel, and endorsement deals. His popularity in social media is staggering. He has 22.8 million subscribers on YouTube, 15 million followers on Instagram, and 5.5 million on Twitter. In August 2019 Ninja jumped from Twitch, where he had 14 million followers, to Mixer, Microsoft's streaming platform, where he has 2.9 million followers.

In December 2019 Ninja and athletic shoe maker Adidas announced the availability of a Ninja-themed blue, black, and yellow Nite Jogger shoe, emblazoned with "Ninja" on the inside of the left shoe and "Time In," the tagline for the partnership, on the inside of the right shoe. It was Adidas's first partnership with a pro gamer. In January 2020, Epic Games, the makers of *Fortnite*, released a custom skin, or graphic that changes the appearance of a gamer's character, featuring an image of Ninja with his trademark yellow bandana and blue hair for fans to buy. Ninja took to Twitter to announce the deal. "I've dreamt of having a skin in *Fortnite* since I started playing the game," the gamer tweeted. "Today, my dream becomes reality."[17]

Jessica Blevins, Ninja's wife and business manager, says that the ability to make brand deals like the ones with Adidas and Epic Games was the real reason for the gamer's move from Twitch to Mixer. "With the wording of how that contract was going, he wouldn't have been able to grow his brand much outside of gaming," Jessica explains. "We were like, 'Straight up, guys, we've worked so, so hard to grow the Ninja brand to license things and get his name out there. We can't go backwards with it.' So that's where that deal just really started not making sense."[18]

Dr DisRespect

After Ninja left Twitch, Florida-based Turner Ellis "Tfue" Tenney became the most-watched lifestyle gamer in the world, with more than 7 million followers on Twitch. Tfue, age twenty-two, is one of the most successful *Fortnite* players in history, having earned more than $500,000 playing the game competitively. In fact, all the top-ten gaming streamers on Twitch now have more followers than Ninja does on Mixer. This includes Herschel "Guy" Beahm IV, a thirty-seven-year-old lifestyle gamer known as Dr DisRespect.

Jessica Blevins (right), Ninja's wife and business manager, says that the ability to make brand deals like the ones with Adidas and Epic Games was the real reason for the gamer's move from Twitch to Mixer.

Beahm wears a 1980s-style mullet wig, sunglasses, and a fake mustache while he plays first-person shooting games, including *PUBG*, *Apex Legends*, and *Call of Duty*. Dr DisRespect entertains his 3.7 million followers by affecting a larger-than-life gamer personality, typified by his popular catchphrases: "I'm on top of the mountain, and I'm only halfway up!" and "Violence. Speed. Momentum." Beahm explains, "I created a character who plays multiplayer video games, and he's considered the most dominating gaming specimen."[19] Personalities like Beahm's creation help keep Twitch gaming and esports popular.

Tiffany Garcia

Men dominate the Twitch top ten, but women are successful lifestyle gamers as well. Tiffany Garcia is one of them. Garcia started uploading gaming videos in 2010, and they have been viewed more than 2 billion times.

Garcia started her career with a series of *League of Legends* and *World of Warcraft* videos, but she became a YouTube superstar after switching to *Minecraft*. Her channel has 6.3 million subscribers, and she holds the record for most video views by a female game broadcaster on YouTube.

Valkyrae

One of the best-known female gamers is Rachell "Valkyrae" Hofstetter, a twenty-eight-year-old *Fortnite* player with close to 1 million followers on Twitch, 856,000 subscribers on YouTube, and 1.8 million followers on Instagram. An advocate for women in gaming, Valkyrae does her best to combat sexism. "Twitch is a mostly male website, so being a female, people come in expecting that I'm going to be taking advantage of that," she says. "Because you know, if you wear a tank top on stream, people will go nuts, regardless of the game or your skill level. I try to stay away from that."[20]

A *Street Fighter* Grandmaster Fights from His Bed

Mike "Brolylegs" Begum is a grandmaster in the game *Street Fighter*. While most elite players make the split-second moves on the Xbox controller with their fingers, Begum makes them by pushing against the inside of his lip with his tongue. He does this because he has limited use of his hands, arms, and entire body. He was born with arthrogryposis, a medical condition that restricts joint movement and inhibits muscle growth. Because of his condition, he cannot walk or even sit up in a wheelchair. Instead, he lies flat on his stomach on a motorized bed that his father custom built for him.

To play *Street Fighter*, Begum holds the controller in his left hand and manipulates it with his face, moving the character with his cheek and executing kicks and other moves with his lip. He competes using Chun-Li, a female character known for her kicking skills. He concentrates on this character because he can only push four of the controller's six buttons, but that is enough to execute all of Chun-Li's moves. Begum mastered the character's moves so well that he was the number one Chun-Li player on Xbox in *Street Fighter IV* from 2013 to 2017. "There's a certain threshold within fighting games where you become pro-player status, world-class, and Broly surpassed that a while ago—he can compete with anybody at this point," says Jonathan "JB" Bautista, the number two–ranked *Street Fighter* player in North America on the Capcom Pro Tour. He and Begum recently teamed up to win $10,000 each in the *Street Fighter* League.

Quoted in Elaine Teng, "Meet Mike 'Brolylegs' Begum: A Most Extraordinary *Street Fighter* Competitor," ESPN, July 10, 2019. www.espn.com.

Nevertheless, Valkyrae, who is one-quarter Hawaiian, one-quarter Japanese, one-quarter Filipino, and one-quarter Puerto Rican, has been harassed by racist and sexist trolls. But they have not discouraged her. "No matter what you do in life, people are going to harass you, so you just have to do your thing anyway,"[21] she says. Valkyrae finds streaming extremely rewarding, not just financially, but emotionally. She says:

> It's just amazing. Streaming is about way more than entertainment. I'm not a pro player, but do a lot of talking and reacting, so people say it's just fun to watch, and it gives them hope that they can play better, or feel better about their playing. . . . I get thousands of emails and messages from people who say I'm helping people with their depression and anxiety, just by playing *Fortnite*. . . . I wouldn't do it for as long as I have, if I didn't realize what an impact it would have on people. I'm just very happy with it.[22]

> "I get thousands of emails and messages from people who say I'm helping people with their depression and anxiety, just by playing *Fortnite*."[22]
>
> —Rachell "Valkyrae" Hofstetter, professional lifestyle gamer

The careers of pro gamers can be long or short. They can make a lot of money or a little, be famous or unknown. But esports is a career that a surprising number of people have succeeded in pursuing. The keys to becoming a pro gamer are to have a passion for gaming, concentrate on a game that offers a pathway to the professional ranks, take constructive criticism, watch and learn from the best, keep fit, practice with a purpose, work on weaknesses even more than strengths to improve overall, and finally, take the big step of entering tournaments where failure is possible, but so is success.

Chapter Three

Building Esports Teams

The rapid growth of esports has created business opportunities that never existed before. Video game publishers expect esports to motivate gamers to stay engaged with the games and buy the new versions as they are released. This market is huge. Newzoo estimates that gamers spent $152.1 billion on video games in 2019, an increase of 9.6 percent over the previous year. Newzoo further estimates that the global video game market will grow to nearly $200 billion by 2022. Advertisers see esports as a way to connect with the coveted young adult market. Gamers themselves view esports as a path to personal wealth. But between these various interests is an opening for a mechanism that can bring them all together, just as a hub connects the various spokes of a wheel. That hub is the esports team.

The Importance of Teams

A team can connect the players with the game publishers, streaming platforms, television networks, advertisers, and merchandisers in a way that generates even more income for everyone, including the team owners. Teams do this by creating more interest in game play than single players can and at the same time negotiating better deals for the players.

Teams appeal to a sense of community and belonging in a way that individual players cannot. Players come and go, but teams endure. Whether it is the New York Yankees, Los Angeles Lakers, Boston Bruins, or Kansas City Chiefs, a professional

The Boston Bruins hockey team participates in a parade in Boston in 2011. Teams appeal to a sense of community and belonging in a way that individual players cannot.

sport team appeals to pride in the community. This shared pride creates a bond with the fans that fuels interest in the teams. Fans spend money to watch their teams perform, to wear their gear, and to buy the equipment they use. The geographic component is at work in esports as well. "Look at the best sports models in the world," says Daniel Cherry, chief marketing officer of Activision Blizzard, the publisher of *Overwatch* and the company behind the founding of the *Overwatch* League. "The most profitable, valuable sports entertainment properties happen to be located in cities that represent a certain geography. So, we're taking that model and we're applying it to eSports. With the *Overwatch* League, we have 20 teams based in major cities across 3 continents."[23]

> "The most profitable, valuable sports entertainment properties happen to be located in cities that represent a certain geography. So, we're taking that model and we're applying it to eSports."[23]
>
> —Daniel Cherry, chief marketing officer of Activision Blizzard

Fan interest, in turn, builds the value of a team. A popular team can charge more money for broadcast rights, advertising, and licensing for branded merchandise. Winning teams often are more popular than losing teams and therefore can make more money. As a result, team owners are willing to pay the best players higher salaries to increase the strength of the team. Competition among the teams to recruit the best players drives up salaries for many pro gamers.

A Magnet for Advertisers

The profit potential of owning an esports team is especially high. Most important, of course, is the growing popularity of esports. Unlike more established sports, esports viewership is growing at a fast rate. Total esports viewership is expected to swell from 454 million in 2019 to 646 million in 2023, an increase of 42 percent, according to financial news website Business Insider. More viewers mean more "eyeballs" that advertisers can reach. As a result, esports broadcasters and streaming platforms can charge advertisers higher rates to access those larger audiences.

The size of the esports audience is not the only factor making it attractive to advertisers. Its age is also important. According to a *Washington Post* survey, almost 60 percent of fourteen- to twenty-one -year-olds have watched a professional gaming tournament. The digital-content provider Limelight Networks reports that people ages eighteen to twenty-five now spend more time watching people play video games online than they do watching other sports. Advertisers are especially interested in reaching a younger audience because young people are still forming loyalties to brands and products. Older viewers may have already decided what soft drinks they enjoy most, what clothing brands they like to wear, and what kind of car they want to drive. Younger viewers are still making up their minds about things and are more open to trying new things. Esports offers a way for companies to reach the youth market.

Not only are Esports fans younger than the general population, they also have more money to spend. According to Newzoo, esports enthusiasts, meaning those who watch esports more than once a month, are more likely to be employed full time than the overall online population is—67 percent versus 53 percent. More esports enthusiasts have higher household incomes than the general online population—43 percent versus 30 percent. These demographics mean that esports enthusiasts have more money to spend on products and services and are therefore a more desirable target audience for advertisers.

The size, age, and relative wealth of the esports audience have attracted enormous amounts of money to the industry. Businesses spent $1.1 billion in advertising, sponsorship, and media rights for esports competitions in 2019. This was an increase of 27 percent over the prior year. The largest share of esports revenues in 2019 was generated in North America—about 37 percent of the global total. China generated 19 percent; South Korea, 6 percent; and Europe and the rest of the world, 38 percent. Newzoo estimates that total global esports revenues will reach $1.8 billion by 2022—an increase of 64 percent over 2019.

The Essence of Esports

Bobby Kotick is the chief executive officer (CEO) of Activision Blizzard, publisher of *Call of Duty*, *Hearthstone*, *Overwatch*, *StarCraft*, and *World of Warcraft*. He met with a group of powerful figures in traditional sports to discuss the potential of professional esports. The group included NFL commissioner Roger Goodell, William Morris Endeavor CEO Ari Emanuel, and three-time American League most valuable player Alex Rodriguez. Kotick was having a hard time explaining how esports differed from traditional sports. He later recalled the breakthrough moment:

> They were asking me where's the sports part? So I asked Alex [Rodriguez] to stand up and I said there are about 1,200 Major League Baseball players and maybe 10 are as distinguished as this guy. Now look at me. There are a billion of me. They want the same sense of belonging and the same sense of purpose and the same sense of meaning. They want their hopes and dreams to be possible and achievable. Those billion people aren't going to get that from traditional sports, but they are going to get it from video games and that's the difference between esports and traditional sports.

Quoted in Arash Markazi, "Column: The Next Major Sport? Josh Kroenke Confident Esports Can Build Big, Global Audiences," *Los Angeles Times*, August 26, 2019. www.latimes.com.

A New and Growing Audience

Because esports enthusiasts are attractive to advertisers, traditional television networks have begun broadcasting esports tournaments. In 2019 ESPN and its affiliated networks—ESPN2, ESPNews, and Disney–ABC Television Group—began broadcasting *Overwatch* League matches. On September 29, 2019, Disney XD aired the *Overwatch* League Grand Finals during prime time—a first for an esport event in the United States. On average, 1.1 million people watched the San Francisco Shock

Loot Boxes and the Value of Promoting Video Games

Most esports tournaments are sponsored by video game publishers as a way of increasing the visibility and popularity of their games. Dedicated gamers not only buy the games, they also purchase accessories, some of which are only available through virtual containers known as loot boxes. Found in popular video games, including *Overwatch*, *Counter-Strike*, and *Fortnite*, loot boxes contain a random assortment of virtual items (loot) to allow players to customize their avatars, or characters, with a custom skin. Some loot helps the players advance through the video game. Players can spend anywhere from $1 to $300 on just one loot box.

Game publishers sell about $30 billion worth of loot boxes each year, according to the technology consultancy firm Juniper Research. Industry analysts estimate that Epic Games, the publisher of *Fortnite*, earns about $300 million a month in loot box sales. With sales like that, publishers can well afford to fund esports tournaments and leagues that keep their products in the news and on the minds of video game customers.

sweep the Vancouver Titans 4–0 on television and online, a 16 percent increase over viewership from the year before. In the important age demographic of eighteen to thirty-four, the *Overwatch* League averaged more viewers week to week than Major League Soccer and Major League Baseball. The 11 percent increase in viewership from 2018 to 2019 was the only increase over all major sports leagues. "Two years [after the *Overwatch* League launched], we're in conversations comparable to the biggest sports leagues in the world,"[24] said Cherry.

TNT also broadcasts esports. In 2016 the network launched *ELEAGUE*, also known as *EL*, as a weekly program that airs live competitions on Friday nights. Unlike the *Overwatch* League, which focuses on only one game, *EL* broadcasts leagues and tournaments for several popular games, including *Counter-Strike:*

Global Offensive, *Rocket League*, *Injustice 2*, *Gears 5*, and *Street Fighter V*. In 2020 the series partnered with Electronic Arts, makers of the *FIFA 20* soccer video game, to host and televise three *FIFA 20* tournaments. The tournaments feature sixty-four of the world's top professional *FIFA 20* players—thirty-two each on the PlayStation 4 and Xbox One consoles—competing for $200,000 in prize money and points, which players use to qualify for the game's ultimate global championship, the *FIFA* eWorld Cup 2020.

EL also hosts celebrity events designed to draw in more casual esports fans. For example, in February 2020, *EL* teamed up with the National Basketball Players Association to hold an *NBA 2K20* esports tournament featuring four NBA players competing for a $10,000 donation to their charity of choice. The tournament featured Zach LaVine of the Chicago Bulls, Rudy Gobert of the Utah Jazz, Shai Gilgeous-Alexander of the Oklahoma City Thunder, and Cam Reddish of the Atlanta Hawks.

A Unique Business Model

Building a successful esports team is different from building other businesses. The owner of an esports team must know how to entice top players to join the team and how to structure player contracts that benefit both the individual and the team. Owners also must know how to negotiate good deals with broadcasters, streamers, and merchandisers. They and their staff must be able to cultivate good relationships with media outlets that can determine how much the public hears about the teams.

Given the unique requirements of being a team owner, it is not surprising that several esports team owners already have a proven track record as team owners in other sports. Stan Kroenke, owner of the NFL's Los Angeles Rams and the NBA's Denver Nuggets, owns the Los Angeles Gladiators, a team in the *Overwatch* League, and the Los Angeles Guerrillas, a team in the *Call of Duty* League. Harris Blitzer, the group that owns the NBA's Philadelphia 76ers and the National Hockey League's New Jersey

Devils, bought the popular esports organization Dignitas in 2016. Dignitas is best known for its *League of Legends* and *Counter-Strike: Global Offensive* teams, but it also fields teams that play *Clash Royale*, *Rocket League*, *Super Smash Bros.*, and *Smite*.

NBA legend Michael Jordan, who is the principal owner of the NBA's Charlotte Hornets, also sees an opportunity to build successful esports teams. He leads a group of investors who invested $26 million in the competitive gaming company aXiomatic Gaming, which owns the popular esports organization Team Liquid, winners of the International in 2017 and runners-up in 2019.

NBA legend Michael Jordan (pictured in 2006) leads a group of investors who invested $26 million in a competitive gaming company that owns the popular esports organization Team Liquid.

Building on Previous Success

Robert Kraft, owner of the multiple Super Bowl–winning New England Patriots and the New England Revolution, a professional soccer team, was one of the seven original owners to pay a $20 million franchise fee to join the *Overwatch* League in 2017. "The incredible global success of 'Overwatch' since its launch, coupled with the league's meticulous focus on a structure and strategy that clearly represents the future of esports made this the obvious entry point for the Kraft Group,"[25] Kraft said, announcing the founding of his new team, the Boston Uprising.

Demonstrating his business savvy, Kraft inked a deal with Gillette, the Boston-based shaving product giant, to sponsor the Boston Uprising in 2018. The Gillette logo now appears on the team's practice jerseys and its new training center. In January 2020, Kraft Group partnered with Helix eSports, which operates esports gaming centers across the United States, to open an 18,000-square-foot (1,672 sq. m) esports complex adjacent to Gillette Stadium, where the Patriots and Revolution play their home games, in Foxborough, Massachusetts. This practice center for the Boston Uprising features one hundred gaming stations with personal computers, gaming and network infrastructure, and thirty public gaming consoles. "Esports is a rapidly growing enterprise and we are thrilled to announce this partnership with Helix eSports to bring this one-of-a-kind facility to Patriot Place for gamers across New England,"[26] said Brian Earley, a vice president within the Kraft Group, announcing the opening of the gaming center.

Stan Kroenke is integrating his *Overwatch* League and *Call of Duty* League teams into his traditional sports teams' venues as well. The esports teams will play in a six-thousand-seat performance hall that is located under the same canopy that covers

> "The incredible global success of 'Overwatch' since its launch, coupled with the league's meticulous focus on a structure and strategy . . . made this the obvious entry point for the Kraft Group."[25]
>
> —Robert Kraft, owner of New England Patriots and the Boston Uprising esports team

45

the seventy-thousand-seat football stadium that serves as the home of the Los Angeles Rams and Los Angeles Chargers in Inglewood, California. Josh Kroenke, Stan Kroenke's son and a co-owner of the Los Angeles esports teams, says:

> We think that few traditional sports can match gaming's reach. The "Call of Duty" franchise has been a best-selling game 10 years in a row, and I have friends who absolutely love playing the game, so I know its popularity is unquestionable. Its fans are some of the most passionate around, and as an esport it's going to be fun to continue to evolve with them alongside the launch of the new league.[27]

The Lure of Competition

Like professional sports team owners, pro athletes and former athletes have a solid understanding of what goes into building a successful professional sports team, albeit from a different perspective. In addition, many pro athletes have a competitive streak that fuels a desire to remain active in the sporting world. Because of these interests and attributes, a few current and former professional athletes are also getting involved with esports ownership. Two-time NBA most valuable player Stephen Curry and his former Golden State Warriors teammate Andre Iguodala are part of a group that invested $37 million in TSM, an esports organization that fields competitive gaming teams for *League of Legends* and *Fortnite*. Pro Football Hall of Fame quarterback and ESPN personality Steve Young was also in on the $37 million TSM investment with Curry and Iguodala.

Curry and Iguodala's former teammate Kevin Durant is also behind an esports team. Durant, who won two NBA champion-

> "We think that few traditional sports can match gaming's reach."[27]
>
> —Josh Kroenke, co-owner of the Los Angeles Gladiators of the *Overwatch* League

Kevin Durant, who won two NBA championships with the Warriors, joined a group that invested $38 million in Vision Esports. Vision Esports owns the esports team Echo Fox.

ships with the Warriors and was the NBA's most valuable player in 2017, joined a group that invested $38 million in Vision Esports, an esports investment fund and management company cofounded by three-time NBA champion and actor Rick Fox. Vision Esports owns the esports team Echo Fox, as well as esports content creator Vision Entertainment and the video game record–tracking site Twin Galaxies. Odell Beckham Jr. of the New York Giants joined Durant in contributing to the $38 million fund-raising round for Vision Esports in 2019. Beckham says he has been an avid gamer since childhood, and he even played against rapper A$AP Rocky in a promotional event for the game *FIFA 19*. The owners of the St. Louis Cardinals baseball team have also invested in Vision Esports. "We have been following the esports sector for several years," says St. Louis Cardinals vice president Dan Good. "In the last year, we have gotten to know the team at Vision Esports and felt this was an exciting investment opportunity."[28]

A Cultural Mash-Up

Esports are a form of entertainment, and members of the traditional entertainment industry are also investing in esports. Like popular athletes, successful show business personalities understand how to cultivate media relations, work with media companies, and even produce branded merchandise. Those with younger fan bases see esports as a way to connect with their fans. For example, in 2018 the Canadian rapper Drake teamed up with Scooter Braun, a Hollywood agent, to become co-owners of 100 Thieves, an esports organization that fields teams that compete in games like *Call of Duty* and *League of Legends*. Drake himself is a gaming enthusiast who played *Fortnite* online with Tyler "Ninja" Blevins. The livestream with Drake and Ninja attracted more than 635,000 concurrent viewers on Twitch.

Actress, singer, and television host Jennifer Lopez was part of a $15 million funding deal for NRG Esports in late 2017. The esports organization has teams in the *Overwatch* League, *Counter-Strike: Global Offensive*, *Hearthstone*, and *Rocket League*. Other investors in NRG include Seattle Seahawks running back Marshawn Lynch, former New York Giants defensive end Michael Strahan, retired New York Yankees infielder Alex Rodriguez, and former Los Angeles Laker Shaquille O'Neal.

Rick Yang, a partner at venture capital firm NEA, focuses on both esports and consumer investing. He believes there is a deep connection between esports and gaming and popular culture that influences consumers. He sees esports as a powerful force that merges competition with other ideas, values, and interests. "I actually think of esports as the mainstreaming of gaming, or the pop culture instantiation [embodiment] of gaming versus the pure idea of these players becoming professionals to compete at the highest levels,"[29] he says. Mariel Soto Reyes, a research analyst at Business Insider Intelligence, the premium research service from Business Insider, agrees with this analysis and believes that esports offers a way to connect with an entire generation of young people. "It's essential to think of the esports opportunity in this way—one inclusive of gaming, media, pop culture, and commerce—as it shines a light on opportunities beyond gaming events alone,"[30] she says.

Soto Reyes believes that looking at esports as simply the intersection of competition and spectatorship "feels like putting blinders on." Instead, she says, people should think of the esports phenomenon as something "that integrates gaming, esports, popular culture, commerce, and the youngest generations." She believes that the social component that comes along with live broadcasts and social platforms, as well as coming together in a stadium to cheer on a favorite team, is what has launched esports into the stratosphere. She points out that esports fans are connected in ways that traditional sports fans are not. "Platforms like Twitch and YouTube Gaming give fans a direct connection to the players and teams," she says. "Everything from the comments sections on streaming platforms, to Instagram and Twitter, plus the advent of the game *Fortnite* which is in itself, arguably, a social platform, have allowed the esports world to go mainstream because of larger audiences having a place and way to connect." In addition, certain esports organizations, such as the American esports and entertainment organization FaZe Clan, are becoming intertwined with people's lives through branding and streetwear. Soto

> "It's essential to think of the esports opportunity in this way—one inclusive of gaming, media, pop culture, and commerce—as it shines a light on opportunities beyond gaming events alone."[30]
>
> —Mariel Soto Reyes, research associate with Business Insider

Reyes believes these connections will go even further, "opening up a world where the fantasies of a video game could be brought to life in some way—think of what a phenomenon *Pokémon Go* was (and still kind of is)."[31] Soto Reyes believes this cultural revolution is just getting started:

> But what's most exciting about taking off the blinders is the fact that I think we're still in the wind-up stage when it comes to esports, video game livestreaming, and the gaming world. There will be events, and maybe even entire theme-park-like experiences built around some of these worlds, and once they include virtual reality and augmented reality we'll see even more yet-unimaginable creations.[32]

Chapter Four

Esports in Education

Video gaming is a participation sport. According to Newzoo, about 2.5 billion people around the world play video games on gaming consoles, desktop computers, or mobile devices. The Pew Research Center reports that 60 percent of US adults aged eighteen to thirty-four and 90 percent of US teens play video games. Friends—in person and online—often form teams to play other teams in pickup games. Other gamers join teams at esports clubs and internet cafés. As the popularity of professional esports has grown, college and high school educators have seen the value of making esports part of a school's curriculum.

The movement is growing. In 2016 only seven colleges had esports teams. By 2020 that number had grown to more than two hundred. The growth in high school ranks is even more astonishing. By 2020 more than thirteen thousand high schools in all fifty states had esports teams. "If college students are the future of the gaming and esports industry, then high school students are the future of the future,"[33] says Mark "Garvey" Candella, director of strategic partnerships at Twitch.

Building a League from Scratch

One of the earliest members of a high-school esports team was Delane Parnell. Growing up on the west side of Detroit, Parnell was never far away from the poverty, crime, and violence that plagues urban communities. "I'm from Detroit. I grew up in the Jeffries Projects. Raised by a single mother. My father was murdered before I was born,"[34] Parnell says. One thing that kept Parnell out of trouble was a competitive video game club run by his high school science teacher. The teacher provided the gaming equipment, kept track of the player stats, and awarded trophies to the winners. "I was super in love with that, and it was probably one of the highlights of my life,"[35] says Parnell.

> "There are 8 million kids today that don't participate in any sports, and there's an opportunity for them to get engaged, develop an affinity for their school, to just be a part of something that's bigger than themselves."[36]
>
> —Delane Parnell, founder of PlayVS

At seventeen, Parnell purchased a wireless phone store and then quickly bought two others. He then founded a car rental service, which soon expanded to sixteen locations across Detroit. He sold the car rental company when he was nineteen so he could concentrate on the technology industry. At twenty he joined a venture capital company, helping Detroit entrepreneurs launch businesses, and at twenty-four he met another tech investor, Peter Pham. Pham encouraged Parnell to build a new company that would bring competitive esports to high schools. Parnell called the company PlayVS, pronounced "play versus."

In November 2017, PlayVS formed an exclusive partnership with the National Federation of State High School Associations (NFHS), which publishes the rules for most high school sports across the United States. The agreement allows PlayVS to provide leagues, scheduling, and infrastructure for high school esports. With the backing of the NFHS, PlayVS was able to reach 19,500 high schools with an officially sanctioned esports program. "There are 8 million kids today that don't participate in any sports, and there's an opportunity for them to get engaged, develop an affinity for their school, to just be a part of something that's bigger than themselves,"[36] Parnell says.

In 2018, at age twenty-five, Parnell sought financial backers for the business in a process known in the venture capital world as a Series A funding round. The company pulled in $15 million from investors that included the rapper Nas, former NBA all-star Baron Davis, Carolina Panthers offensive tackle Russell Okung, and the NFL's San Francisco 49ers. It was the largest Series A ever raised by a black founder in the consumer internet industry. Just five months later, in November 2018, PlayVS raised another $30 million from investors, including rapper Sean "Diddy" Combs and Elysian Park Ventures, the private investment arm of the Los Angeles Dodgers ownership group. Ten months later PlayVS raised another $50 million in funding, bringing the company total to $96 million in just fifteen months.

To make the platform even more appealing to students, PlayVS has struck up partnerships with video game publishers to bring popular games to the high school level. These games include *League of Legends*, *Rocket League*, and *Smite*. By 2020

Video gaming is a participation sport. As the popularity of professional esports has grown, college and high school educators have seen the value of making esports part of a school's curriculum.

PlayVS had formed high school esports leagues in all fifty states, with more than thirteen thousand schools participating and eighty thousand students playing.

An Inclusive Activity

PlayVS is not the only high school esports organization. Founded in 2018, the High School Esports League (HSEL) oversees programs in more than twenty-five hundred schools with more than seventy-five thousand participants. The league offers competition in ten different games. These include the six-versus-six team game *Overwatch*; the five-versus-five games *Counter-Strike: Global Offensive* and *Rainbow Six: Siege*; the three-versus-three game *Rocket League*; the two-versus-two game *Call of Duty: Modern Warfare: Gunfight*; the one-versus-one games *Super Smash Bros. Ultimate*, *Hearthstone*, *NBA 2K20*, *Madden 20*, and *FIFA 20*; and solo games *Fortnite* and *Minecraft: Survival Games*.

> "About half of our kids that go out aren't involved in any other sport or extracurricular. We felt like that was kind of a neat opportunity for them to get involved and connect with other kids."[37]
>
> —Brian Unruh, Cedar Falls director of instructional technology

School administrators see esports as a way of enhancing the high school experience for students who are not involved in traditional sports or other activities. "The more we looked into it, the more we liked the idea and being able to really provide an opportunity for kids that might not have been involved in other extracurricular activities in school," says Brian Unruh, director of instructional technology in Cedar Falls, Iowa. "About half of our kids that go out aren't involved in any other sport or extracurricular. We felt like that was kind of a neat opportunity for them to get involved and connect with other kids."[37]

School-sponsored esports involves more than playing video games. It places video gaming within a structured group environment that helps develop interpersonal skills, just as other team sports do. "It brings people together and when they're working together, it's like any other team sport," explains Jackie Albarella,

How to Start a School Esports Team

On its website, the High School Esports League (HSEL) offers a step-by-step guide about how to start a varsity esports team:

#1 Find a teacher who will be able to help you manage your team and schedule meetings. Many teachers already mentor clubs (such as robotics, gaming, anime, etc.) and they can be a great resource to reach out to for starting your team. If you can't find a teacher willing to help, reach out to a school activities member for direction.

#2 Find interested students to join the team. Get the word out about your team with posters or flyers, or talk to other students about the team during club day at your school. Remember that a team with all types of members is important—it isn't necessary to love games to play esports.

#3 Develop a plan with your teacher advisor. Work together to plan out meeting days and times, and to finalize any paperwork your school may need to make your team official. Start the HSEL partnership application.

#4 Reach out to interested students about the finalized team meeting days and times. We suggest creating an email list with emails from each student to keep in touch. Make a Discord, Facebook Group, or Twitter to streamline communication. Plan out some topics for the first meetings to keep things on track. Your teacher advisor can help with this.

#5 Contact interested students and host your first team meeting. Once your club is up and running, you can start delegating leadership and working on team building activities. We suggest meeting multiple times a week for practice and to improve teamwork.

#6 Get partnered with HSEL! . . . Participate in national tournaments and win prizes.

High School Esports League, "After School Partnership Program," 2020. www.highschoolesportsleague.com.

an animation and design teacher at Bennett High School and the International Preparatory School in Buffalo, New York. "They're all for each other. We're trying to also teach them compassion and good sportsmanship and that's what we're infusing with video games." Esports can be more inclusive than traditional sports are. "It's a team sport that any student can get involved in," says Albarella. "You don't have to be the biggest, you don't have to be the fastest, you don't have to be the tallest, and you can be a member of an eSports team."[38]

An Academic Tie-In

As with traditional sports, the thrill of competition and the life lessons learned by winning and losing are the main benefits of organized esports. And like traditional sports, esports have benefits outside the playing arena. Like professional gamers, student gamers develop their bodies as well, learning about good nutrition, wellness, and even physical activities such as stretching that can improve their performance.

Like traditional sports, esports have benefits outside the playing arena. Student gamers learn about good nutrition and physical activities such as stretching that can improve their performance.

Esports are even easier than traditional sports to integrate into the academic curriculum. Many esports programs are sometimes interdisciplinary. For example, an English course can examine the narrative qualities of a particular game. Math and computing courses can delve into the strategies of the games. "The same kinds of skills you need for a STEM career are all embraced in eSports,"[39] says Albarella.

The HSEL has even developed an accredited semester-long course that teaches STEM and other life skills through the lens of video games and esports. Developed by Kristy Custer, principal of Complete High School Maize in Maize, Kansas, and Michael Russell, a social studies teacher at the same school, the course, called Gaming Concepts, covers gaming appreciation, motor skills, careers in gaming, maintaining healthy practices, self-management, goal-setting and decision-making skills, and interpersonal communications.

According to the HSEL, students who took the course in a pilot program improved their grade point averages by an average of 1.4 points, and attendance increased from 85 percent to 95 percent. "Students with chronic absenteeism who do not feel a connection to the school especially benefit from esports,"[40] says Custer. She adds:

> As an administrator, I'm always looking for new ways to engage students in school. Online gaming is helping us achieve this goal. We are not reinventing the wheel here. Many, if not all of our students, are already spending time playing games. We are just providing some intentionality in the focus of what they are doing, as well as providing context where their gaming can support their academic and career goals in an engaging and creative way.[41]

> "It's a team sport that any student can get involved in. You don't have to be the biggest, you don't have to be the fastest, you don't have to be the tallest, and you can be a member of an eSports team."[38]
>
> —Jackie Albarella, animation and design teacher at Bennett High School and the International Preparatory School in Buffalo, New York

Another K–12 esports program, known as EliteGamingLIVE, also links gaming to related academic activities, including coding, audio and video engineering, and virtual reality. "We don't tell kids that they should be a professional video gamer," says Kerwin Rent, founder of EliteGamingLIVE. "Every company that sells something is going to need people that engineer those experiences. These are all things that are really important in the world of gaming that people get paid a lot of money to do."[42]

Esports in Higher Education

At the collegiate level, esports is less about interdisciplinary education and improving attendance and more about making a name for the school, in the same way that successful National Collegiate Athletic Association (NCAA) football and basketball programs increase the visibility of winning universities. "The college views this as an enrollment and retention strategy," says Molly Mott, associate provost at State University of New York at Canton, which competes with about forty other colleges in *Hearthstone*, *League of Legends*, *Overwatch*, *Fortnite*, *FIFA*, *Rocket League*, and *Super Smash Bros. Ultimate*.

Because esports is new, all schools—big and small—have an equal chance of building a successful program. And because esports teams are small, schools do not need huge budgets to compete. However, this situation might not last long. "We have to move as quickly as we can to differentiate ourselves and to build a reputation," says Eric Darr, president of Harrisburg University, located in Harrisburg, Pennsylvania, which sponsors a top-ranked esports team. "In some sense, [the goal is to] become the Notre Dame of esports—a smaller, private, independent [university] that can keep pace and, on any given day, beat the big guys."[43]

David Versus Goliath

Darr and his school triumphed in September 2019. The Harrisburg University Storm faced off against the Ohio State University Buckeyes in the semifinals of the Harrisburg University Esports

A Degree in Esports

Shenandoah University, a private university in Winchester, Virginia, has begun to offer a degree in esports. The major was the idea of Joey Gawrysiak, a professor and the university's esports director. He started teaching classes in video games in 2015 and then helped launch the school's esports team in 2018. With the backing of the student senate, he met with video game publishers Blizzard Entertainment and Riot Games about the practical experience students would need to enter the industry and designed a curriculum to meet those needs. The degree is not about becoming a professional gamer but about how to run and plan esports events. Tracy Fitzsimmons, the college president, was skeptical of the idea at first, but she eventually supported it. She explains:

> They mapped out how the academic program could be rigorous and there would be jobs available for students upon graduation. . . . We have also found that adding esports has created a welcome opportunity for new partnerships with technology companies and sports management venues. This program straddles Shenandoah's strengths in business, performing arts and athletics.

Quoted in Jeremy Bauer-Wolf, "Video Games: Entertainment or Sports?," Inside Higher Ed, February 12, 2019. www.insidehighered.com.

Invitational, a competition that included sixty-four teams from thirty-five colleges competing in *League of Legends*, *Hearthstone*, and *Overwatch*. Ohio State has a student body of more than 66,000 undergraduate and graduate students and an NCAA Division I athletic program with a budget of $175 million. Harrisburg, by contrast, has a student body of just 6,469 and no traditional varsity athletics programs. Nevertheless, Harrisburg's *League of Legends* team defeated Ohio State's team 2–1 to proceed to the tournament finals.

The Ohio State gamers did take away some positive memories from the tournament. In the quarterfinals, the twelfth-seeded Buckeyes upset fourth-seeded Robert Morris University, from Chicago, Illinois, in the quarterfinals, 2–1. Then in the semifinals against Harrisburg, the Buckeyes shocked the home team by winning the first game, handing Harrisburg its first loss of the tournament. The Ohio State gamers then went on to build up a big lead in the second game, and it looked like they might close Harrisburg out. But the Storm rallied, staging a dramatic comeback to win. "I think a few of us just choked in that game," said Daniel "Icelandic Hero" Helgason, a player for Ohio State. Nevertheless, Helgason took solace in knowing that his team had pushed Harrisburg to the limit. "Afterward I heard that Harrisburg had to pull out their secret strategy for Game 3 because they could not risk saving it for finals,"[44] he said. Perhaps because it was forced to deploy its secret strategy in the semifinals, Harrisburg fell to Maryville University in the finals.

A Number One Team

Maryville University, with an enrollment of ninety-two hundred students, is another small school that is having an outsize impact on collegiate esports. Located 22 miles (35.4 km) from downtown St. Louis, Missouri, Maryville founded its esports program in 2015. Just one year later, the school won its first *League of Legends* College Championship. The Saints successfully defended their title in 2017 and won it for the third time in four years in 2019. "We are proud of our student-athletes who lead the collegiate Esports arena," said school president Mark Lombardi after Maryville defeated Western University of Ontario, Canada, 3–0 in the 2019 *League of Legends* finals. "Their hard work and determination has put our Esports Program on the map."[45]

Lombardi is right. Maryville was ranked number one in the preseason ESPN College *League of Legends* coaches poll. "The Saints are the reigning College *League of Legends* champions and a perennial powerhouse in the collegiate scene,"[46] ESPN

stated, explaining its ranking. Harrisburg University was ranked number three in the ESPN poll, Western Ontario was number five, and Robert Morris was number eleven. Ohio State came in at number twenty-four.

Maryville University team players (five players on the left) are seen with members of a college team from China (right) at the 2019 League of Legends *International College Cup final. Maryville won the title for the third time in four years.*

Scholarship Programs

One of the reasons that Maryville and Harrisburg have enjoyed so much success in esports is that they have invested in recruiting top esports talent. Both schools were among the first universities in the nation to offer scholarships to esports student-athletes. Each of Harrisburg's twenty-six esports team members receive a full-tuition scholarship and a housing stipend. This esports deal exceeds what many collegiate programs offer traditional athletes. Collectively, colleges offered more than $15 million in esports scholarships in 2019. "The competitive leagues offer scholarships to help students pay for college," says Christopher Turner, the esports coach at Southern University Laboratory High School in

Baton Rouge, Louisiana. "Nowadays, colleges offer Esports programs for students, which creates a new viable path to college for those who may never have considered obtaining a higher education."[47]

To remain on the esports teams, the Harrisburg gamers must participate in mandatory physical training sessions, adhere to strict meal plans, attend study hall, take part in four-hour daily practices, and maintain a 2.0 grade point average on a full load of courses. "Our team here is no different than my experience I had as a college athlete," says Ryan Korn, a university employee responsible for the school's high school partnerships program. "I had a full [scholarship] for football. The experiences [that players] have with regards to training, with having the work-life balance between their sport and college . . . that's how it was for me."[48]

In addition to the scholarships, Harrisburg spends about $2 million a year on its esports teams, covering coaching and staff salaries, facilities, technology, travel, and hosting events. In addition, the school is spending $750,000 to build an on-campus, elite gaming facility.

Some of the big schools are starting to upgrade their esports programs, too. In 2018 Ohio State announced that it would build a dedicated esports arena and conduct research initiatives aimed at improving gaming performance. The involvement of well-known schools is viewed by some as further legitimizing collegiate esports. "I love that Ohio State is diving in," says A.J. Dimick, esports director at the University of Utah. "It helps moves the needle in the right direction."[49]

Obstacles to Esports

Despite their growth and popularity, collegiate esports face obstacles to becoming as large of an enterprise as traditional sports. One reason is that the NCAA, the governing body of traditional collegiate athletics, does not sanction esports. This is because NCAA regulations forbid student-athletes from accepting money for anything related to their sports activities, including cash prizes, product endorsements, gifts, or extra benefits that have a monetary value. These regulations would disqualify many of the best esports players. Elite esports gamers typically compete for and win cash prizes in tournaments while they are in their teens, even before they go to college. In addition, many top players receive money from advertising on their streaming platforms, fan donations, and sponsorships. None of these things are allowed under NCAA rules.

In April 2019 the NCAA board of governors voted unanimously not to get involved with overseeing esports. In addition to questions about the amateur status of elite gamers, the NCAA also has concerns about how the content of certain video games matches up to NCAA values. For example, many of the top competitive video games are centered on violence—first-person shooting, third-person shooting, hand-to-hand fighting, and military combat. "We know that some of the content is really violent," says NCAA president Mark Emmert. "We don't particularly embrace games where the objective is to blow your opponent's head off."[50]

Emmert and others at the NCAA are also concerned about the depiction of women in video games that are played competitively. While female figures in video games are typically courageous warriors capable of amazing feats, they often are depicted in revealing outfits—costuming not shared by male characters. This sexual objectification can create a hostile learning environment for female gamers as well as spectators. "We know a lot of the content is hugely misogynistic," says Emmert. "We know there are serious concerns about health and wellness around those games."[51]

Emmert is hopeful that the NCAA can use its leverage to influence the video game publishers to make the games less violent and sexist. "We may have an opportunity in front of us to apply our values to esports and better align those games to our values to change not just what happens in our activities but what happens across your campuses and more broadly what happens in society," Emmert says. "We don't want to ever change our values to fit a game or some other entity. We want to change that entity to fit our values."[52]

Another challenge involves Title IX of the Education Amendments of 1972, a federal law that protects against gender discrimination. Currently, 95 percent of esports players are male, according to Emmert. Title IX compliance requires a school to make sure the proportion of male and female athletes matches the proportion of the student body overall. "[Gender diversity] is a very real concern,"[53] says Justin Camputaro, director of the University of Washington's Husky Union Building, the home of the school's esports arena. He continues:

> Unfortunately, we do not have as good of answers to this. Right now we are focused on talking about this a lot with the gaming student organizations and talk about a grass-roots environment of being open and welcoming. [We're] also actively encouraging women that the space and gaming is welcome to them. However, what we cannot control is the online arena where players are in other places that do have negative talk against women. This topic is one that we have agreed to tackle head on over this next year, especially as we build out a competitive program, to focus on co-ed [gaming] and inclusivity.[54]

Ellen Staurowsky, a professor of sports management at Drexel University in Philadelphia, Pennsylvania, and a Title IX expert, believes that collegiate esports should not let the NCAA hamper its growth. By staying outside the NCAA, the collegiate esports players can continue to earn money from donations, sponsors, and video streaming, as they would from any other off-campus jobs. In addition, the schools can advertise their esports programs in ways the NCAA would not allow, attracting new students and building partnerships with video game publishers and other tech companies.

With or without NCAA backing, collegiate esports is destined to grow far into the future. The video game industry was built on an entrepreneurial spirit that already is transforming high school sports and esports. The new programs, in turn, are bringing gamers together in ways that many never thought possible. Jason Chung, a visiting clinical assistant professor at New York University's Preston Robert Tisch Institute for Global Sport, believes that esports is a force for good in the lives of students. He writes, "By embracing esports, schools can capitalize upon its organic growth and draw students away from uninteractive, sedentary avenues of entertainment towards an activity that can instill common values and principles."[55]

"By embracing esports, schools can capitalize upon its organic growth and draw students away from uninteractive, sedentary avenues of entertainment towards an activity that can instill common values and principles."[55]

—Jason Chung, visiting clinical assistant professor at New York University

Source Notes

Introduction: A Human Drama

1. John Jewell Balan, interview with the author, February 7, 2020.
2. Quoted in Dian Schaffhauser, "Free Esports Curriculum Contains Full Lesson Plans," The Journal, September 13, 2019. https://thejournal.com.
3. Quoted in Robin Miller, "A National Title Is Within Reach for Southern Lab Esports League Gamer Timotheus Moore," The Advocate, December 12, 2019. www.theadvocate.com.
4. Quoted in Nick Schwartz, "ESPN's President Says That Esports Are Not 'Real Sports,' and He's Wrong," *USA Today*, September 6, 2014. https://ftw.usatoday.com.

Chapter One: A Global Phenomenon

5. OG (@OGesports), "Against all odds, we stood united, fought until the very end and became your #TI8 Champions!," Twitter, August 25, 2018. https://twitter.com.
6. Quoted in Will Partin, "'StarCraft II': How Blizzard Brought the King of Esports Back from the Dead," *Variety*, July 13, 2018. https://variety.com.
7. Joona Sotala (@ENCE_Serral), "Yess!! Managed to pull it off," Twitter, August 5, 2018. https://twitter.com.
8. Quoted in Reuters, "Drini Shuts Out Spoto 41–0 to Win Madden Bowl," ESPN, April 28, 2019. www.espn.com.

Chapter Two: Inside the World of Pro Gamers

9. Quoted in Vlad Savov, "Inside the Life of a Pro Gamer," The Verge, July 21, 2014. www.theverge.com.

10. Quoted in Tonya Predco, "[EN] WESG 2016 Americas Finals: Interview with ExpScarlett," YouTube, October 24, 2016. https://youtu.be/Zc0cQdg2_WM.

11. Quoted in Hector Rodriguez, *OpTic Gaming: The Making of eSports Champions*. New York: HarperCollins, 2016, p. 5.

12. Quoted in Maddy Myers, "How Pro Gamers Live Now: Curfews, Personal Chefs, and All of It on Camera," Kotaku, June 21, 2018. https://compete.kotaku.com.

13. Quoted in Bloomberg, "The Glamorous Life of a Pro Gamer," YouTube, June 21, 2018. https://youtu.be/35YXuEXDa20.

14. Quoted in Myers, "How Pro Gamers Live Now."

15. Quoted in Myers, "How Pro Gamers Live Now."

16. Quoted in Bloomberg, "The Glamorous Life of a Pro Gamer."

17. Ninja (@Ninja), "I've dreamt of having a skin in *Fortnite* since I started playing the game," Twitter, January 15, 2020. https://twitter.com.

18. Quoted in Dave Smith, "Jessica Blevins, the 27-Year-Old Manager and Wife of the Most Popular Video-Game Player in the World, Reveals the Inside Story of Ninja's Move to Microsoft's Mixer," Business Insider, October 2, 2019. www.businessinsider.com.

19. Quoted in Darin Kwilinski, "The Doc Will See You Now—Meet the Mind Behind Dr DisRespect," ESPN, November 10, 2017. www.espn.com.

20. Quoted in Kaylee Fagan, "This 26-Year-Old *Fortnite* streamer Says She Paid Off Her Mom's Debt with Her Twitch Earnings," Business Insider, June 11, 2018. www.businessinsider.com.

21. Quoted in Fagan, "This 26-Year-Old *Fortnite* Streamer Says She Paid Off Her Mom's Debt with Her Twitch Earnings."

22. Quoted in Fagan, "This 26-Year-Old *Fortnite* Streamer Says She Paid Off Her Mom's Debt with Her Twitch Earnings."

Chapter Three: Building Esports Teams

23. Quoted in Bruce Rogers, "CMO Daniel Cherry III Leading Activision Blizzard into ESports Future," *Forbes*, July 24, 2019. www.forbes.com.
24. Quoted in Alex Stedman, "*Overwatch* League's Grand Finals Grows 16% in Average Viewers from Last Year," *Variety*, October 3, 2019. https://variety.com.
25. Quoted in Todd Spangler, "*Overwatch* League Initial Teams Unveiled: Patriots, Mets Execs Among Esports Franchise Owners," *Variety*, July 12, 2017. https://variety.com.
26. Quoted in Catherine Carlock, "Kraft Group to Open Esports Arena at Patriot Place," *Boston Business Journal*, November 14, 2019. https://www.bizjournals.com.
27. Quoted in Arash Markazi, "Column: The Next Major Sport? Josh Kroenke Confident Esports Can Build Big, Global Audiences," *Los Angeles Times*, August 26, 2019. www.latimes.com.
28. Quoted in Jacob Wolf, "Echo Fox Ownership Group Vision Esports Raises $38 Million," ESPN, February 22, 2018. www.espn.com.
29. Quoted in Mariel Soto Reyes, "Esports Ecosystem Report 2020: The Key Industry Players and Trends Growing the Esports Market Which Is on Track to Surpass $1.5B by 2023," Business Insider, December 18, 2019. www.businessinsider.com.
30. Soto Reyes, "Esports Ecosystem Report 2020."
31. Mariel Soto Reyes, interview with the author, March 23, 2020.
32. Soto Reyes, interview.

Chapter Four: Esports in Education

33. Quoted in Mykal Vincent, "Newly-Founded Esports Club at SU Lab Raising Money for Gaming Computers, Equipment," WAFB 9, September 12, 2019. www.wafb.com.
34. Quoted in Melia Robinson, "High Schoolers Across America Will Start Playing Video Games for Sport This Fall—Meet the 25-Year-Old Detroit Native Who Made It Happen," Business Insider, April 7, 2016. www.businessinsider.sg.

35. Quoted in Matt Perez, "This 25-Year-Old Has Nas and the 49ers Investing in High School Esports," *Forbes*, June 4, 2018. www.forbes.com.
36. Quoted in Perez, "This 25-Year-Old Has Nas and the 49ers Investing in High School Esports."
37. Quoted in Nick Petaros, "Collaborative Effort Lifts Cedar Falls to a National Esports Championship," *Waterloo-Cedar Falls (IA) Courier*, December 26, 2019. https://wcfcourier.com.
38. Quoted in Ryan Zunner, "Esports Teams Coming to Buffalo High Schools," WBFO NPR, December 18, 2019. https://news.wbfo.org.
39. Quoted in Zunner, "Esports Teams Coming to Buffalo High Schools."
40. Quoted in Schaffhauser, "Free Esports Curriculum Contains Full Lesson Plans."
41. Quoted in Melany Moncav, "High School Esports League Partners with Kansas School District," Esports Insider, September 20, 2018. https://esportsinsider.com.
42. Quoted in Brooks Dubose, "Maryland Turns to Esports to Push Students Toward STEM," Center for Digital Education, November 20, 2019. www.govtech.com.
43. Quoted in Alex Andrejev, "This Small Pennsylvania School Wants to Be the Notre Dame of Esports," *Washington Post*, October 16, 2019. www.washingtonpost.com.
44. Quoted in Aaron Lien, "Esports: Ohio State Places Fourth at Harrisburg Invitational," *The Lantern* (Ohio State University), September 23, 2019. www.thelantern.com.
45. Quoted in Maryville University, "Maryville University League of Legends Team Wins Third National Championship in Four Years," May 28, 2019. www.maryville.edu.
46. ESPN, "Maryville University No. 1 in Preseason ESPN College League of Legends Coaches Poll," January 17, 2020. www.espn.com.
47. Quoted in Vincent, "Newly-Founded Esports Club at SU Lab Raising Money for Gaming Computers, Equipment."
48. Quoted in Andrejev, "This Small Pennsylvania School Wants to Be the Notre Dame of Esports."

49. Quoted in Noah Smith, "Ohio State is Latest Power Conference School to Embrace Esports While NCAA Sits Idle," *Washington Post*, October 11, 2018. www.washingtonpost.com.
50. Quoted in Tom Schad, "NCAA Tables Possibility of Overseeing Esports," *USA Today*, May 21, 2019. www.usatoday.com.
51. Quoted in Schad, "NCAA Tables Possibility of Overseeing Esports."
52. Quoted in Tim Reynolds, "NCAA's Mark Emmert Expresses Concern over Sports Betting, Esports," *Las Vegas (NV) Review-Journal*, January 24, 2019. www.reviewjournal.com.
53. Quoted in Eric Stoller, "An Epic Update on Collegiate Esports," Inside Higher Ed, May 16, 2019. www.insidehighered.com.
54. Quoted in Stoller, "An Epic Update on Collegiate Esports."
55. Jason Chung, "High Schools Need to Get Over It and Embrace Esports," *Wired*, October 10, 2019. www.wired.com.

For Further Research

Books

Paul Chaloner, *This Is Esports (and How to Spell It): An Insider's Guide to the World of Pro Gaming*. London: Bloomsbury Sport, 2020.

William Collis, *The Book of Esports*. New York: Rosetta-Books, 2020.

Roland Li, *Good Luck Have Fun: The Rise of eSports*. New York: Skyhorse, 2016.

Hector Rodriguez, *OpTic Gaming: The Making of eSports Champions*. New York: HarperCollins, 2016.

Ryan Rogers, ed., *Understanding Esports: An Introduction to the Global Phenomenon*. Lanham, MD: Lexington, 2019.

Scholastic, *Esports: The Ultimate Guide*. New York: Scholastic, 2019.

Internet Sources

Alex Andrejev, "This Small Pennsylvania School Wants to Be the Notre Dame of Esports," *Washington Post*, October 16, 2019. www.washingtonpost.com.

Jason Chung, "High Schools Need to Get Over It and Embrace Esports," *Wired*, October 10, 2019. www.wired.com.

Brian Feldman, "The Most Important Video Game on the Planet," *New York*, July 9, 2018. http://nymag.com.

Arash Markazi, "Column: The Next Major Sport? Josh Kroenke Confident Esports Can Build Big, Global Audiences," *Los Angeles Times*, August 26, 2019. www.latimes.com.

Maddy Myers, "How Pro Gamers Live Now: Curfews, Personal Chefs, and All of It on Camera," Kotaku, June 21, 2018. https://compete.kotaku.com.

Bruce Rogers, "CMO Daniel Cherry III Leading Activision Blizzard into Esports Future," *Forbes*, July 24, 2019. www.forbes.com.

Mariel Soto Reyes, "Esports Ecosystem Report 2020: The Key Industry Players and Trends Growing the Esports Market Which Is on Track to Surpass $1.5B by 2023," Business Insider, December 18, 2019. www.businessinsider.com.

Websites

Esports Charts (www.escharts.com). Esports Charts provides detailed, up-to-the-minute statistics about all esports tournaments and leagues, including current and past year schedules, viewership of events, viewer hours, and much more. It offers easily searchable information on teams, organizers, platforms.

GosuGamers (www.gosugamers.net). GosuGamers offers news articles about the latest esports happenings. It lists recent esports events, tournaments, and matches going on around the world and even provides links to the livestreams when these are available.

High School Esports League (www.highschoolesportsleague .com). The High School Esports League oversees esports programs in more than twenty-five hundred schools with more than seventy-five thousand participants. It also offers accredited esports curriculum materials. The website provides ways for schools to join leagues and compete with other schools.

Liquipedia (http://wiki.teamliquid.net). Created and maintained by the members of Team Liquid, a popular esports multigaming organization, this site serves as an online encyclopedia for all things related to esports. It includes rosters (and roster changes) of esports teams, tournament listings, and match results.

PC Gamer (www.pcgamer.com). *PC Gamer* is a print magazine and website that covers PC games. The website includes gaming news, features, esports coverage, hardware testing, and game reviews.

PlayVS (www.playvs.com). PlayVS offers schools software that lets them join esports leagues, schedule meets, and keep statistics on their school's esports program. The website offers a step-by-step guide to helping a school set up an esports team. It also offers a pathway for individual students to compete in solo games.

Index

Picture Credits

About the Author

Bradley Steffens is a poet, a novelist, and an award-winning author of more than fifty nonfiction books for children and young adults.